Diverse Workforces and Investigative Report Writing
Essential Knowledge for Business Leaders

Louis Bevoc

I0402607

Published by
NutriNiche System LLC

For information contact:
info@nutriniche.com

Louis Bevoc books...simple explanations of complex subjects

Diverse Workforces

Challenges and Benefits of Age, Race, Religion, Handicaps, Gender, Gender Identity, and Sexual Orientation

Louis Bevoc

Published by
NutriNiche System LLC

For information contact:
info@nutriniche.com

Louis Bevoc books...simple explanations of complex subjects

Introduction

The business world employs a wide variety of people who differ in appearance, personality, beliefs, and viewpoints. This variety is partially due to organizational leaders realizing the value of a diverse workforce, but it is also a natural result of the global marketplace. People from the same companies are employed all over the world; thereby turning those companies into global meting pots that continuously add new workers into the mix.

There are many books on workplace diversity that exist today. Most of these books provide valuable information and facts that educate and inform people about the struggles diverse employees face. However, few books discuss the benefits they provide…and those benefits need to be highlighted and brought to the forefront.

This book focuses on employee age, race, religion, handicaps, gender, gender identity, and sexual orientation. It examines the challenges these individuals face as well as the value they add to organizations. It does not take a stance on any aspect of these people's employment, but it does provide information that can be used by readers to draw their own conclusions. The text is informational and educational, and it is written for easy understanding at any reader level….which is the premise of all Louis Bevoc books.

Now that you understand the scope of this book, let's move forward. The first section focuses on older employees.

Age

Without a doubt, workforces around the world are aging (or ageing as it is spelled in some areas of the world). In fact, over one-quarter of people working today are 50 or older. This is rather astonishing, especially in the United States, because it could not have been predicted back in 1935 when the Social Security Act was instituted. Part of this act was designed to protect elderly people's health and welfare after they were no longer capable of protecting themselves. However, in 1935, people rarely worked after they reached their mid-sixties…but times have changed. For a variety of reasons, including longevity and financial concerns, people are choosing to work longer…something that will not likely change in the near future.

Some people refer to the term "silver tsunami" for the aging population of today. Quite simply, this term means there is a large mass or wave of older people living today. Their longevity is due to health awareness and modern technology, and some of them have chosen to remain in the workforce; thereby resulting in higher numbers of older employees than have ever been seen in the past.

Not surprisingly, aging employees face challenges that are typically not encountered by their younger coworkers, but they also add value when those younger coworkers are unable to do so. Some of the major challenges and benefits of hiring older workers are discussed below.

Challenges of hiring

Older workers are often stereotyped in the minds of their younger coworkers. Many of those stereotypes are unfair and wrong, but others might actually be true including those listed below.

Flexibility- Older employees are often thought of as rigid or set in their ways. They have done things a certain way for many years, and that way is the only way and the right way. In some instances, this perception might be true, but it is not completely valid. If given the chance, many older employees will gladly change. If they see a better way to do something, then they will be the first to adhere to that way. However, like it or not, some older workers lack flexibility.

Absenteeism – Older people are known to show up for work when they are physically able, but they also miss work due to health-related issues. It can be said that everyone has some type of health concern, but older workers typically experience injuries, disease, and sickness more than younger employees because the human body weakens as people age. For example, very few employees under the age of 30 worry about heart problems because young people rarely experience heart attacks. However, workers over age 55 are concerned with heart problems because the chance of them having a heart attack is much greater. Heart problems, and measures taken to prevent heart problems, can require time off from work; thereby making absenteeism a challenge of hiring older workers.

Technology – Possibly the biggest challenge faced by older employees is technology. Technological advances are constantly occurring and they can be difficult to keep up with for all employees...especially those who are older and might be a bit resistant to change. Younger workers tend to embrace new technology because they grew up with constant change and upgrades. However, this embracement might fade as they are constantly bombarded with new concepts. Older employees have been there and done that...and that is why they often find technology to be challenging.

Training – This challenge is related to technology because training is often conducted for technological reasons. When technology changes, older employees typically require more education than those who are younger. Training is beneficial because people learn how to do their jobs effectively and efficiently. However, training also costs money...and more training means more spending. In short, training has a monetary impact on the bottom line, which causes business leaders to use caution when hiring older workers.

Benefits of hiring

Older employees also provide advantages to their employers that are rarely provided by younger workers. Some of their major benefits are discussed below.

Experience – More and more business leaders are realizing that experience is critical for the growth and prosperity of their organizations. This experience comes from personnel who understand workplace goals and objectives and know what it takes to achieve them. Nobody understands workplaces better than those who have worked in them for long periods of time. They know what works and, more importantly, what does not for solving problems. In short, experience makes older workers beneficial for hiring.

Political understanding – Experience is important for understanding the best way to perform job functions, but it also has other value. It helps people interact with coworkers and, sometimes, more importantly, it helps them understand the dos and don'ts of workplace politics. Like it or not, every workplace has some type of political atmosphere that must be navigated for employees to be successful. Experience is critical for this navigation because veteran employees are not new to workplace politics. They understand the issues that can result and how to deal with those issues. Most people who have encountered workplace politics are well aware of the negative effects they can have on workforces...and having someone around who can reduce or eliminate those effects is a huge bonus.

Knowledge sharing – Older employees are often willing to share their knowledge because they are not threatened by younger workers. Their willingness is due to them no longer having the desire to climb the corporate ladder and the fact that the information they share is valued. In short, older workers often act as mentors to younger employees so those employees can further their own careers.

Loyalty and reliability – Older employees are typically hard working and honest because they are loyal to the organizations that employ them. They can also be relied upon to show up for work and, contrary to what some people might believe, they usually have a very good work ethic. In short, they take pride in what they do and their loyalty and reliability make them a plus for the organizations that hire them.

Race

Race is a very touchy subject inside and outside of workplaces. There are written and unwritten rules in place about what can be said and what type of behavior is acceptable. However, as the business world progresses so do the needs of organizations...and the inclusion of different races is an important aspect of those needs.

Workforces with different races face some challenges that are not encountered by workforces made up of homogenous employees. However, diverse workforces also have advantages over homogeneous workforces due to their makeup. Some of the major challenges and benefits of hiring older workers are discussed below.

Challenges of hiring

Hiring people of different races appears to be a great idea because the workforce turns into a melting pot of ideas from different perspectives. However, a racially diverse workforce does encounter some challenge including those listed below.

Communication – Communication is challenging in just about every workplace, but an extra dimension is added when employees of different races do not speak the same languages. For example, some Hispanics speak Spanish while whites and blacks often speak English. If this language differential is present, then it can easily create a barrier to communication in workplaces.

Customs, culture, and slang also have the potential to distort communication between employees. For example, some Asians do not look directly into the eyes of their bosses out of respect. However, those bosses can be offended if they see this as a lack of interest. Additionally, some blacks put a high value on the respect they receive at work, while whites do not always share the same viewpoint. Most employees are able to overcome these differences, but the point is that they do exist and they can distort communication.

Training – This challenge often results from the lack of communication that occurs in workplaces. Quite simply, a lack of understanding results in the need for employees to be educated, and education needs to come in the form of training. Training is good for improving workplace learning and understanding, but it is also expensive. For cost reasons, most business leaders would prefer not to train their workforces.

Political correctness – Race probably impacts political correctness more than anything else in workplaces. Employees need to be careful about what they say and how they word their thoughts to avoid offending those who are different. The reasoning behind political correctness makes good sense, but it does present a challenge when hiring people of different races.

Division – "Birds of a feather flock together" is a phrase that means people with a common interest will be found together. Sometimes this is good, such as when two football teams are playing against each other in an important game. However, it is not always good in companies because new thoughts and ideas become restricted to a particular way of thinking. In short, if races of employees stick with their own rather than interacting with those that are different, then a division results that stifles the creative process necessary for the growth and prosperity of organizations.

Benefits of hiring

As astute business leaders are aware, companies that hire different races of employees find the diversity beneficial. Some of these benefits are as follows:

Idea generation – Ideas are critical for organizational growth and prosperity. In fact, companies that do not generate new ideas typically do not survive because their competition moves forward while they stagnate and regress. Different races have different thoughts and viewpoints that take creativity to a higher level and play a major role in the generation of new ideas. These ideas help grow existing market share and, more importantly, help companies compete in new markets that previously did not exist due to a lack of diverse thinking.

Viewpoints – No two people think alike, and there are no concrete predictions of how anyone is going to react to the situations that they find themselves in. Their reactions are driven by viewpoints, and viewpoints often differ based on race. If only one race exists in a company, then that race's viewpoints will likely drive the way that company conducts business. There are little if any challenges to the status quo; thereby preventing organizational growth. In short, differing viewpoints are needed in organizations in order to make the best decisions, and multi-racial workforces provide those viewpoints.

Global appeal - Without a doubt, companies with multi-race workforces companies are more appealing on a global level than those that only employ one race. This is because people all over the world want to see a little of themselves represented in the organizations that supply their products and services. Quite simply, companies that lack multi-racial workforces might be successful on a local level, but that success will be met with resistance when they move into the global marketplace.

Empathy – When races come together in organizations, it is natural for them to develop an understanding for each other. This understanding stems from the fact that they have to work together and start to learn about each other's personal lives. They realize that they share common interests and experience similar problems as they move through life. When this happens, barriers are broken down, stereotypes go by the wayside, and discrimination that once existed is no longer found. In short, different races develop empathy for each other based on real experiences rather than bias, fear, or hearsay.

Religion

The global marketplace that exists today has resulted in diverse workplaces all over the world. Employees from these workplaces come from a variety of different countries and backgrounds. An important part of those backgrounds often involves religion and the beliefs that accompany it. Workforces with a variety of religious beliefs can be advantageous due to the diverse thinking that exists, but employees within those workforces can also enter into conflict that is not good for them or their organizations.

Some of the major challenges and benefits of hiring workers who follow different religions are discussed below.

Challenges of hiring

As some employees can likely attest to, there are challenges with hiring people who have strong religious beliefs, and some of these challenges are listed below.

Rigidity - Some people have religious beliefs that they will not deviate from regardless of the setting. They simply cannot leave their personal thoughts at home; thereby causing their religious beliefs to spill over into the workplace. An example is the thinking that homosexual relationships are wrong. Men should not be with men, and women should not be with women because these types of relationships are not approved by their religious organizations. Religious individuals are entitled to their beliefs and opinions, but those beliefs and opinions should not be brought into the workplace.

Friction - Friction can occur in any workplace, but is most likely present when some employees dislike the behavior of others. Unfortunately, religious behavior is particularly troubling for certain people. For example, atheist employees might despise the fact that religious workers refer to their faith while performing their jobs. These atheists consider religious talk and references to be "hogwash" and this creates friction between them and the religious employees.

Discomfort – Employees who do not understand certain rituals that go along with religion can be taken out of their comfort zones. They do not know what to say or do, and this unknowingness interferes with the completion of required job tasks. In extreme situations, the discomfort experienced can cause tension in the air can be "cut with a knife."

Perception – This refers to the perception of unfairness when religion interferes. Employees who need time for prayer might be viewed as getting special treatment by those who do not require that time. This negative perception can demotivate workers and, in more extreme cases, cause them to seek employment elsewhere.

Benefits of hiring

On the flip side of the coin, there are advantages to hiring those with strong religious affiliations, and some of these advantages are listed below.

Devotion – Religious people are often devoted to their faith, and that devotion tends to spill over into their jobs. Devoted workers are willing to "go the extra mile" to get things done; thereby making their coworker's jobs easier because those coworkers get the help they need to complete their own tasks. Quite simply, astute business leaders strive to hire devoted employees because they know those employees will do their best to achieve organizational goals and objectives...and sometimes that devotion is found in people who embrace religion.

Faith – Religions are based on faith, and many times that faith includes the thinking that people are basically good. If employees believe people are basically good, then they will believe in their coworkers and managers. Positives rather than negatives will be assumed about others' actions; thereby resulting in a harmonious workforce that strives to accomplish the same goals.

Structure – People who believe in their religion are willing to adhere to the policies and procedures established by those religions. They follow rules set forth by those in power and understand their roles as members of their congregations. Many times their religious behaviors follow them to their jobs; thereby helping them adhere to rules and understanding their roles as employees of organizations. In short, religious workers are often willing to follow the structure that is in place...and this makes them beneficial to the companies that hire them.

Respect – One of the best ways to maintain good relationships with coworkers is to respect them as individuals and employees.

When there is a lack of respect, people tend to not want to work with each other and job tasks do not get completed. Religious employees tend to understand the value of respect based on the teaching of their faith, and that understanding is important for organizational growth and prosperity.

Handicaps

This refers to employees with mental or physical handicaps. These individuals have some type of impairment that prevents them from performing at the same level as other employees, but that impairment does not prevent them from completing job tasks with a little help. In fact, companies that employ people with handicaps typically get workers who are dedicated and hardworking, but those workers are sometimes unable to do their jobs without some type of aid (physically handicapped) or make important decisions about their jobs (mentally handicapped).

Unfortunately, handicapped workers often face unjustified discrimination. It can be argued that discrimination is a concern for any employee who is different from the norm, but it is a major issue for handicapped people because some employees fear working with them. Coworkers believe the disabled person will not be able to think and react to problems as they arrive, even though this might not be true. For example, a person in a wheelchair is able to brainstorm as well as anyone else. Their physical disability does not affect them mentally even though there might be a misconception that it does due to their appearance and need for help in some situations.

Handicapped employees have found employment in many different industries and they are applauded for their work, but they also have personal needs that can affect others in their workplaces. Some of the major challenges and benefits of hiring handicapped employees are discussed below.

Challenges of hiring

They are some challenges with hiring handicapped individuals, and some of these are listed below.

Modifications – Normal work environments can be difficult for handicapped workers to navigate due to the obstacles they face. For example, employees in wheelchairs might need to move to various levels of a shop floor to perform all of their job functions. If this is the case, then a ramp needs to be installed. That ramp is a modification that requires money and time to complete.

Flexibility – This challenge applies to mentally and physically handicapped workers. These employees are not as flexible as others because they have limitations that prevent them from doing so. For example, mentally handicapped workers might find it difficult to be part of a job rotation program because it takes them longer to learn.

Speed – Most handicapped people work at a slower pace than their non-handicapped coworkers, and this pace reduction is understandable due to the restrictions involved. For example, a machine might need to be run at a lower speed to accommodate mentally handicapped people who cannot make fast decisions about how to proceed. Along the same lines, physically handicapped individuals might not be able to move as freely as others; thereby requiring the same machine to reduce its speed.

Learning curves – This challenge affects mentally handicapped employees who have difficulty learning at the same rate as other workers doing the same jobs. These individuals might be completely capable of performing the required functions of their jobs, but they have to be shown how to perform those functions over and over. Their extended learning curve ties up time and money that could be used elsewhere.

Benefits of hiring

As might be expected, there are advantages to hiring handicapped employees. Some of these advantages are listed below.

Retention – This benefit often goes unnoticed because it does not always stand out even though it is very important. Handicapped employees tend to remain with their organizations longer than other workers because they value their jobs more than those other workers. They appreciate the fact that their employers had enough faith in them to hire them into a job that might require modified workplaces or longer learning curves. Employee retention is a goal for every organization, and handicapped workers help achieve that goal.

Safety – Past studies, including one from DuPont, have found that handicapped workers are involved in fewer accidents than non-handicapped workers. This is good for employers because injuries, costs, and OSHA visits are reduced. In fact, safety issues make up some of the biggest problems encountered by companies today...and handicapped employees help to mitigate those problems.

Financial incentives - Some companies that employ handicapped people qualify for tax credits. This means they are essentially paid for the jobs they provide to people with mental or physical challenges. This is great because employees and organizations benefit. In short, handicapped employees are a benefit because they create win-win situations via financial incentives.

Government requirements – Interestingly, some companies with federal contracts are now required by law to employ people with disabilities. The number of people employed is based on a percentage that is noted in the Rehabilitation Act of 1973. This makes hiring handicapped people a benefit that could positively influence the bottom line. So, businesses that are affected by the Rehabilitation Act might find that it works to their advantage.

Gender

Some people would argue that gender-neutral people exist in workplaces, but most would agree that the two basic genders of employees are male and female. Traditionally, males have dominated the top positions in the organizational hierarchy, but this is changing. Women are now CEOs of companies all over the work, and their presence continues to grow and prosper. However, by no means does this mean that discrimination against women in the workforce is non-existent…it simply means that times are changing in terms of diversity, and women are leading the way.

This section focuses on women in the workplace because they are still a minority. Like many other diverse groups of people, they have benefitted businesses worldwide, but they also have needs that affect themselves and their coworkers. Some of the challenges and benefits of hiring women employees are discussed below.

Challenges of hiring

The following are some challenges associated with hiring female employees:

Attendance – Like it or not, women are typically the main caregivers for children. This might not be fair because men should play an equal role, but it is often a reality. It also means that women need to take time off work when their children need them because other caregivers are not legally allowed to do some things necessary for children, and they are not willing to do other things…such as care for kids when they are sick. Unfortunately, motherly necessities can make attendance a challenge for employers who hire female employees.

Flexibility – This refers to job flexibility…something that is very important for people in general. However, personal commitments, often related to family (children and parents), put job flexibility at the top of the need's list for some women. They want to work at times that fit their schedule, but their schedules do not always fit the needs of their employees; thereby making job flexibility a challenge for employers hiring women.

Bias – This challenge should not need to be discussed, but it is a reality in some organizations due to the "good old boy" mentality that lingers on. One might think that solely viewing women in clerical or non-management positions is a thing of the past, but, unfortunately, this is not always the case. Some employees, especially those who are older and have experienced their share of male-dominated leadership, believe women have their place in companies...and that place is not in higher up positions.

Obviously, bias is wrong and does not make good business sense, but it does occur and it can be a challenge associated with hiring women.

Desire – This refers to the lack of desire to progress within organizations. Quite simply, some women do not want to obtain high positions in their companies regardless of the fact that they might be the most qualified. They have other aspects of their life that take precedence, and they do not care if that precedence causes them to lose out on the top jobs. This challenge is also applicable to men, but it is more prevalent when hiring women due to their more frequent roles as caregivers.

Benefits of hiring

The following are some advantages that companies experience when hiring women employees.

Multitasking – Arguably, women are better at multi-tasking then men. This is because they typically focus on more roles than men...including family and socialization calendars. They know how to juggle multiple responsibilities while achieving goals and objectives; thereby making them beneficial to the companies that hire them.

Team builders – Women tend to be open to other's thoughts, ideas, and opinions...which is something that many men struggle with. This openness creates a much more diverse way of thinking that leads to innovative concepts and ideas. Along the same lines, women are often more willing than men to share responsibilities for completing tasks. In short, they are generally not predisposed to control everything, and this mindset leads to better decision-making.

Compassion – Women are often more compassionate than men in life and at work. This might sound misogynistic or stereotypical, but it is true in many cases. However, this trait is a good one to have at work because employees feed on compassion in order to perform at their highest levels. People need their coworkers to feel their problems and relate to their pain, and compassion addresses that need…which is why women are a benefit for organizations that hire them.

Emotional intelligence – Emotional intelligence is someone's ability to manage their own feelings and understand the feelings of others. It is essential for getting along with others in workplaces…and women often find that it is naturally within them. They are empathetic and understanding, and they have the ability to actively listen to what others are saying. This is by no means saying that men are not emotionally intelligent; it is simply saying that this trait is more innate in women…which is why they are beneficial for organizations that hire them.

Gender identity and sexual orientation

These types of diverse employees are saved for last because they are the most complex, and possibly least understood, of all employees. Gender identity and sexual orientation essentially refer to LBGT employees. LGBT is an initialism that is gaining popularity to the extent that it is now known by the masses. It stands for lesbian, gay, bisexual, and transgender people who live and work with straight (heterosexual) individuals. These individuals have come a long way in terms of being included in straight communities, but the fight for acceptance is far from over.

Gay pride events, including parades and festivals, have increased acceptance of LGBT people by bringing their lifestyles into the mainstream. These events expose straight individuals to alternative lifestyles; thereby reducing the stereotypes that are present during LBGT closet-based activities. The key here is reducing the fear of the unknown that causes people to react negatively to things they do not understand or have not personally experienced.

However, regardless of the efforts to promote acceptance, the LGBT community is not always understood by the straight community. This lack of understanding flows outside of personal lives and into workplaces all over the world.   In fact, it might be more prevalent in people's jobs than it is in their personal lives regardless of the fact that there are laws in place to prevent discrimination. This might be because straight people can avoid interaction with the LGBT community in their personal lives, but they are forced to interact with them in work-related situations. In some instances, this forced interaction can result in straight people becoming more understanding; thereby reducing stereotypical barriers that tend to hinder workplace productivity. However, it can also result in the furthering of stereotypes that add to existing bias rather than reducing or eliminating it.

Everyone faces hurdles that they need to overcome in order to find success in their working careers, but those hurdles are typically based on work-related issues that do not follow a person from job to job. LBGT employees are unique because they face the same controversy regardless of where they work or the job they are performing. However, that controversy also makes them stronger as individuals which can be advantageous for their employers. Some of the major challenges and benefits of hiring LBGT employees are discussed below.

Challenges of hiring

There are challenges with hiring LBGT, and some of these are listed below.

Discomfort – Employees with unique gender identity and sexual orientation can cause discomfort among coworkers if that identity or orientation is known. However, that level of discomfort can be even higher if a coworker is unaware and says something that might be perceived as wrong or offensive. For example, employees who engage in telephone conversations are not able to display the visual and non-verbal cues used during face-to-face communication. In most cases, this lack of cues does not present any problems because people are able to communicate their thoughts and ideas verbally. However, telephone conversations are not always easy for LBGT people...especially those whose voices do not match the gender that defines them. A man who becomes a woman might have a deeper sounding voice and be mistaken as a man by the person on the other end of the telephone. This mistake is not a major cause for alarm because it was unintentional, but it can cause discomfort on both ends. The LBGT person might not feel comfortable making a correction, and the offending person might be embarrassed after they find out that they have made a mistake.

Acceptance – Some workers cannot find it within themselves to accept the lifestyle of LBGT employees. They might or might not openly display their feelings, but, regardless of the openness, those feelings exist and can be harmful. As noted earlier, LBGT employees identify as being lesbian, gay, bisexual or transgender. However, this identification is not always openly exposed to their coworkers due to fear of the hostility or lack of acceptance that might transpire. Sexual identification in workplaces is also kept secret due to a "don't ask, don't tell" atmosphere...which has historically been the norm in the military. In the minds of some LBGT employees, honestly is not always the best policy.

The identity challenge can be particularly troubling for LGBT personnel when their coworkers are constantly whispering among one and other about what they think might be true. Gossip and rumors are present in every workplace, but sexual preferences always seem to be at the top of the list. Not surprisingly, LGBT employees are often targets of discussion behind their backs...and this type of treatment can prevent them from focusing on the work aspects of their jobs. The time they spend worrying about what has been said about them is counter-productive in terms of accomplishing work-related tasks, and this results in them not doing their jobs to the best of their abilities....which makes hiring them a challenge.

Support – This challenge refers to lack of support, but not from employees. It refers to the lack of support from management. In many cases, management is unsure how to handle situations involving LBGT employees, so they withdraw and do nothing. Since doing nothing usually does not result in anything constructive or positive, it is rather easy to see why lack of support is a concern. Business leaders who realize that they might not support LBGT employees often find it challenging to hire them.

Socialization – Many people have said that they are not at work to make friends. This might be true in some instances, but, in reality, it is usually not the case. Solid personal relationships at work are typically needed because people are willing to help others they like personally. Without those relationships, work is hindered, and, in some cases, does not get completed. For LBGT employees, establishing personal relationships with their coworkers can be challenging…even to the point where they look elsewhere for employment. For this reason, hiring LBGT employees can be challenging for organizations.

Benefits of hiring

Below are some advantages of hiring LBGT workers:

Resilience – One thing most people would likely agree on is the fact that LGBT people are resilient. This makes sense because they are typically less understood than any other types of employees. They are used to having to work hard and get past stereotypes at home and in the workplace. Practice makes perfect, and LBGT people practice resilience on a regular basis…which is why they are beneficial for companies that hire them.

Openness to change –Change is going to happen in organizations whether people like it or not. It has to occur because, without it, companies would become stagnant and fail to grow. Over time, lac, of growth challenges an organization's ability to exist and might very well cause it to close its doors for good. LBGT employees are less resistant to change than others because many of them have made major changes for a good part of their lives. They knew their lifestyles might offend others, but they still moved forward, rolled with the changes, and found success personally and professionally. Based on their openness to change, LBGT employees are beneficial to the companies that hire them

Lack of fear – In order to make it in the business world, people needs to able to "fall off the horse and get back on again." They cannot be afraid of making a mistake or looking bad in front of their coworkers or they will find it difficult to succeed. LBGT people typically do not fear making a mistake or failing at something because they have faced adversity for much of their lives. They fear the unknown less than others because they have been down that path...which makes them valuable employees.

Driven – Many employees are driven to succeed because they want to experience the rewards from that success. They know they will encounter obstacles, but they will not let those obstacles stop them. LBGT employees are a step ahead of their coworkers in terms of finding success because they have experienced many challenges, yet they remain determined to accomplish goals and objectives. Their experiences make them stronger when workplace obstacles surface, and they continue to move forward. Without a doubt, LBGT employees benefit their employers because they are driven to succeed without feeling defeated or giving up.

Summary

Workplace diversity is more of a reality today than it has ever been in the past due to the expansion of the global marketplace. Business leaders are realizing the advantages diversity offers, but they also know that those advantages must overcome the challenges that come with them.

This book explores workplace diversity. It examines employee age, race, religion, handicaps, gender, gender identity, and sexual orientation by focusing on the challenges these individuals face as well as their value to organizations. The text is educational and informational, and it is written for easy understanding at any reader level.

Congratulations! You now understand more about the challenges and benefits of diverse workplaces...an increasingly popular topic that is discussed in organizations all over the world.

Investigative Report Writing
In Organizations

Louis Bevoc

Published by
NutriNiche System LLC

For information contact:
info@nutriniche.com

Louis Bevoc books...simple explanations of complex subjects

Introduction

Most people who have written a report for school know that it can be a tedious and difficult task. Research has to be conducted, facts need to be discovered, and information needs to be well written and accurate. School reports are important because they help determine the final grades students receive upon completion of the course. However, a report written for a class is not nearly as important as one written for a rape, beating, or murder because there are victims who, if they survive, can be damaged emotionally, psychological, and/or physically for the rest of their lives.

This book is about reports that are not as important as those for violent crimes, but often carry more importance than school reports. They are known as investigative reports, and they take place in organizations for a variety of reasons including injury, theft, accidents, damage, harassment, intimidation, discrimination, and other incidents that that occur in workplaces. These reports need to be written properly so all pertinent facts and information are documented, but, more times than not, they are written with inaccurate or missing facts and information. Common errors include those listed below.

- Facts are missing or inaccurate.
- Times and dates are missing or inaccurate.
- People who are involved are not interviewed.
- Interviews are not in-depth.
- Interviewers do not ask the right questions.

Obviously, the above list is not complete, but it does show how report writing can be inaccurate. If reports are inaccurate, then wrong conclusions can be drawn and decisions regarding those conclusions can be unjust. This book shows how to write detailed investigative reports that have measures in place to prevent facts and information from being inaccurately entered or omitted.

Before moving into specific sections of investigative report writing, it is important to understand these reports have been written for many years. However, based on the legal aspects involved with workplaces today, the content of the reporting has become much more detailed. That content takes all related factors into consideration while documenting detailed facts about the allegation. Information is typically gathered qualitatively and it is used to make a quantitative analysis. For example, in the case of sexual harassment, the investigator needs to interview the accuser, accused, witnesses, and anyone else who knows something about the alleged incident. In terms of interviewing, more is better because common denominators and general consensus can be extracted. This process of interviewing large numbers of people is known as qualitative information gathering. That information is then analyzed and a conclusion is drawn. In the case of sexual harassment, the conclusion is a decision that determines whether the accused is guilty or not guilty of the accusation. This decision-making process is quantitative because it provides an exact answer.

Now that you understand the concept of investigative report writing and the premise of this book, let's move forward into the process of how these reports are written.

Report writing

Each section is shown below beginning with the Executive Summary.

Executive Summary

A discussion on the executive summary is somewhat premature at this point, but it is important to understand what it is and why it exists. Quite simply, an executive summary provides an image of the incident that took place for everyone that needs to know what happened. It is typically placed at the beginning of the report, but it is not written until the report is finished.

An executive summary is very important. In fact, it is sometimes the most important aspect of an investigative report because readers make decisions to stop or continue reading based on it. In short, it provides a snapshot of the alleged behavior or wrongdoing, the investigation of that alleged behavior or wrongdoing, and the outcome of that investigation. If done correctly, an investigative summary is all the reader needs to obtain a basic understanding of the report and its findings.

Example

On November 23, 2018, Andover Industries received a complaint from a wheelchair-confined handicapped worker, Bob Mills, who claimed he was being harassed. Specifically, Bob said that Nick Williams called him "retard" and "Mr. Efficient" causing him to become embarrassed, angry, demotivated, and non-productive.

On November 24, 2018, I, Ralph Johnson, interview Mr. Mills and three different witnesses who supported his claims. Mathew Houghton, Trish Danielson, and Lyn Presnal all stated that this harassment has been ongoing for the past few months.

I interviewed Mr. Williams on November 26, 2018, and he admitted he had made "a few comments" over the past week, but he denied making these comments for the past three months. He also stated that his comments were made jokingly and everyone viewed them as "light-hearted humor."

Based on my interviews, I substantiate Mr. Mills' claim of harassment. I recommend Mr. Williams be required to undergo the diversity acceptance training offered by our human resources department. I also informed Mr. Williams that a copy of this written report would be available for him by November 29, 2018.

The section following the Executive summary is known as the Opening.

Opening

Essentially, the opening section encapsulates important information regarding the investigation in a concise manner in terms that everyone can understand. The introduction to the Andover Industries' report is as follows:

Complaint identifier

CC441-10

Date of complaint

November 23, 2018

Accuser

Bob Mills

Accuser work information

Hire date – June 17, 2006
Position - Sander
Department – Finishing
Plant – Holman Technology
Supervisor – Roscoe Tillman
ID – 2113P

Accuser personal information

Address –
21455 Alexander St.
Avon Lake, OH 44012
DOB – 9/12/81
Phone - 216-221-4725
Work phone – Not applicable
Fax – Not applicable
Email - bob.mills@gmail.com
Work email – Not applicable
Social media – NA
Spouse – Erica Mills

Accused

Nick Williams

Accused work information

Hire date – October 22, 2015
Position - Grinder
Department – Finishing
Plant – Holman Technology
Supervisor – Roscoe Tillman

Accused personal information

> Address –
>> 29001 Redstone Court
>> Apt. 211
>> Cleveland, OH 44015
>
> DOB – 8/17/93
> Phone - 216-515--3756
> Work phone – Not applicable
> Fax – Not applicable
> Email - nickwill93@hotmail.com
> Work email – Not applicable
> Social media –
>> Twitter - @nickwill93
>> Facebook - Nick Williams
>
> Spouse – Not applicable

Investigator

> Ralph Johnson
> Human Resource Manager
> Holman Technology
> 3400 Richdale Rd.
> Cleveland, OH 44109
> Email - ralph.johnson@andover.com
> Work phone - 216-774-2300 X - 3775
> Work fax - 216-774-2500

The opening provides some details that are not listed anywhere else in the investigative report. It provides information about the accuser, accused, and investigator for a basic understanding before moving into the rest of the report.

The next section is known as the incident, and it provides some specifics about the accusation and situation.

Incident

This is the section where the investigator describes what happened. The incident to the Andover Industries' report is as follows:

What is the accusation?

The accuser (an employee) alleges workplace harassment by the accused (a coworker).

Who is the accuser?

Bob Mills

Who supervises the accuser?

Roscoe Tillman

Who is accused?

Nick Williams

Who supervises the accused?

Roscoe Tillman

What are the specifics of the accusation?

In reference to the Andover Industries' report, the incident is as follows:

Bob Mills, a sander in the finishing department at the Holman plant, alleges that Nick Williams, a grinder in the finishing department at the Holman plant, has called him derogatory names on several occasions. Bob says that he put up with the harassment until it became unbearable; thereby affecting him psychologically and causing him to lose focus on his job responsibilities.

Now it is time to narrow the focus of the investigation, and this is done in the scope section.

Scope

This section of the report lists all the steps in the investigation. The scope for the Andover Industries' report is as follows:

> This investigation focuses on a complaint filed by one employee against another employee. The alleged victim, alleged accuser, and three witnesses are interviewed to obtain details on the situation. Those details will be used to piece together what really happened and determine if the alleged complaint is legitimate.

Now we can move into the interviews section. This is where most of the important information for the report is obtained.

Interviews

This section discusses every interview taken during the investigation. It essentially asks those involved to share their versions of the situation by discussing people involved, happenings, dates, times, statements, conversations, and behaviors. It is the most detailed section in the report, and it is useful for scrutiny or challenges that might arise later on.

The interviews for the Andover Industries' report were conducted in person by Ralph Johnson, Human Resource Manager at Holman Technology. Ralph asked the interviewees to provide their name, job, employee ID, and length of employment along with a detailed description of what happened on November 23, 2018.

On November 24, 2018, five employees were interviewed including Bob Mills, Nick Williams, Mathew Houghton, Trish Danielson, Lyn Presnal, and Roscoe Tillman. Please note the following regarding these interviews:

- All interviews were voluntary.
- All interviews took less than ten minutes to complete.
- All statements provided were signed by the interviewees.

- None of the employees had to be re-interviewed.

The interviews are listed below.

Bob Mills (accuser)

> I am Bob Mills, employee ID 2113P, and I work for Andover Industries as a Sander in the finishing department at the Holman plant. I have worked for Andover Industries for 12 years including 5 years at the Saddle Design and 7 years at Holman Technology.
>
> On November 23, 2018, at about 1:00 pm, Nick William made fun of me by calling me a "retard" due to the fact that I am confined to a wheel chair and need help maneuvering when performing my job duties. Specifically, another employee needs to operate a lift when I need to sand machinery at levels that I cannot reach from the ground. I was offended by this and told nick that I am very capable of doing my job to the satisfaction of my boss, Roscoe Tillman, but all he did was grin and say "you are right, so I will call you Mr. Efficient."
>
> Nick has made fun of me in the past, but this time I was very upset and decided to file a harassment complaint with human resources at the Holman plant. I filed the complaint because I was so mad that I could not focus on my job responsibilities and believed something needed to be done to stop Nick from insulting me.

Nick Williams (accused)

> I am Nick Williams, employee ID 4229P, and I am employed at the Andover Industries' Holman Technology plant as a Finisher in the Finishing Department. I have worked for Andover Industries for 3 years at the Holman plant.

On November 23, 2018, at about 1:00 pm, I made fun of Bob by calling him "retarded," and he went to HR to complain about my comment. The fact of this matter is that I was completely joking, and Bob knew I was joking. We kid back and forth all the time, so I don't know why this time is such a big deal. He has said stuff to me in the past, but I have never filed a complaint. This situation has been blown way out of proportion by Bob and everyone else. This company is way too sensitive about kidding around and, in this situation, a "mountain is being made out of a molehill."

Mathew Houghton (witness)

I am Matt Houghton, employee ID 2006P, and I work for Andover Industries as a Sander in the Finishing Department at the Holman plant. I have worked for Andover Industries for 14 years at Holman Technology.

On November 23, 2018, at about 1:05 pm I witnessed Nick Williams call Bob Mills a "retard." Bob became upset and said something to Nick that I could not hear. He then looked even angrier and said he was going to Human Resources to file a complaint.

Trish Danielson (witness)

I am Trish Danielson, employee ID 9225L, and I work for Andover Industries as Inventory Control Specialist in the Inventory Department at the Holman plant. I have worked for Andover Industries for 4 years at Holman Technology.

On November 23, 2018, at about 1:00 pm I heard Nick Williams call Bob mills a "retard," causing Bob to get mad. Bob told Nick he did not want to be called names and abruptly walked away. I did not know where Bob was going, but he was moving quickly. After Bob left, Nick thought the situation was funny.

Lyn Presnal (witness)

I am Lyn Presnal, employee ID 9811Q, and I work for Andover Industries as a Quality Assurance Technician in the Quality Department at the Holman plant. I have worked for Andover Industries for 2 years at Holman Technology.

On November 23, 2018, at about 1:00 pm I witnessed Nick Williams call Bob mills a "retard." I did not hear Bob's response, but he said something back to Nick while Nick laughed at him. Bob then said he was going to human resources and stormed off.

Roscoe Tillman (supervisor of accused and accuser)

I am Roscoe Tillman, employee ID 1744P, and I am employed at the Andover Industries' Holman Technology plant as the Finishing Supervisor in the Finishing Department. I have worked for Andover Industries for 28 years including 6 years at the Prevention Controls facility and 22 years at Holman Technology.

I did not witness the situation between Bob Mills and Nick Williams, but Bob told me in the past that he would prefer not to work with Nick. When I asked him why he did not want to work with Nick, he said it was due to "personality differences" that did not involve the job. I tried to separate Bob and Nick as much as possible, but they work in the same department, sometimes on the same jobs, so keeping them apart all the time is not practical.

Now that the problem has been defined and the witnesses' accounts of what transpired have been documented, it is time to move forward. The next section analyses the information available so a decision can be made about the innocence or guilt of Nick Williams.

Analysis

I, Ralph Johnson, conducted the entire analysis.

I found that all three of the witnesses' stories corroborated; thereby determining that their stories must all be accurate. This finding of accuracy is further supported by the fact that all three witnesses have never been written up or disciplined for anything while employed at Andover Industries. In short, they are employees in good standing with the company.

I also believe that there have been problems between Bob Mills and Nick Williams based on my interview with their supervisor, Roscoe Tillman. He tried to keep these two apart, but their separation is not in the best interest of Andover Industries, so his decision to have them work together in certain instances is justified. Roscoe only has one write-up during his employment at Andover, and that was for attendance issues in 1994, so his testimony is further supported due to his good standing with the company.

The only story I found to be false is that from Nick Williams because he was the only person with this version of the story. Nick does not believe his behavior was offensive or abusive, but he is clearly wrong based on the no harassment policy that Andover Industries has had in place since 1995. Nick Williams has two previous write-ups documented on his record in the 3 years that he has worked here. He unsuccessfully argued that he was not guilty in both instances; thereby raising questions about his truthfulness in this situation.

Conclusion

Based on my analysis, I find that Bob Mills' allegation that Nick Williams harassed him is true. Mr. Williams' behavior fits the definition of harassment as defined in the Anderson Industries' employee handbook, and there is no "grey" area that warrants discussion.

This report and its findings will be passed to Henrietta Kowalski, Director of Human Resources for Anderson Industries, and she will decide what type of disciplinary action, if any, will be taken against Nick Williams.

Recommendations

The findings of this investigation show that harassment exists in the workplace at Anderson Industries. We should benefit from this incident by incorporating measures that will help prevent harassment in the future. I recommend mandatory diversity training for all employees at least once per year. This training will highlight the differences between employees and offer ways to help our workers accept those differences. Additionally, question and answer sessions should be available for employees who are unsure of what is expected of them in terms of diversity acceptance.

Review

Regardless of how good your report might be, it is critical to review it before submitting to others. The following should be considered:

- Were any pertinent facts left out? Is anything missing? Were all "rocks uncovered?"
- Were all witnesses interviewed? Did anyone else see what happened? If so, can they be located and interviewed?
- Is the conclusion bias? Is the investigative report writer honest and sincere? Is there any type of discrimination?
- Were all relevant factors taken into account? Did the accuser have a reason to go after the accused? Was the accused targeted?
- Were the circumstances taken into account? Did the accused or have mental health problems, excessive stress, physical illness, or something else that caused them to do what they did?
- Are there any spelling or grammatical errors? Do these errors make the writer look careless? Should the report be edited by a professional?
- Does the report need to be reviewed by attorneys? Is the report safe from a legal standpoint? Is it possible that a lawsuit could result?
- Is the report stored in a secure place? Is it only assessable to authorized people? Can unauthorized people view it?

All of the above questions need to be considered in order to write a well-written, unbiased, and accurate report. A thorough review could prevent mistakes that end up leading to other problems...including legal action.

Summary

Investigative reports are written every day in organizations all over the world. They are created for many different reasons, but they all have in common the fact that that they are used to document actions, draw conclusions, and make decisions. Without investigative reports, "he said, she said" situations would run rampant.

This book focuses on the process of investigative report writing. It defines and describes all relevant sections including the Executive Summary, Opening, Incident, Scope, Interviews, Analysis, Conclusion, and Recommendations. The text is informational and educational, and it is written for easy understanding at all reader levels.

Congratulations! You now understand more about how to write investigative reports...documents that are often necessary for the efficient operation of businesses.